Crazy Jane

Crazy Jane

poems

Pat Falk

Plain View Press
P. O. 42255
Austin, TX 78704

plainviewpress.net
sb@plainviewpress.net
1-512-441-2452

Copyright Pat Falk, 2007. All rights reserved.
ISBN: 978-1-891386-95-4
Library of Congress Number: 2007941820

Cover Art: *Barbara by the Fire*, detail from *Dreamscape in Red and Black* by CB Follett.

Photo of poet by Lawrence Chatterton.

Acknowledgments

Grateful acknowledgment is made to the following publications in which some of these poems have appeared, at times in altered form: *And What Rough Beast: Poems at the End of the Century; For Loving Precious Beast; 13th Moon; The Light of City and Sea; Live Poets Volume 4; Long Island Quarterly; Long Island Sounds; The Muse Strikes Back; The Nassau Review; Petroglyph; Off the Cuffs; The Pedestal Magazine; Songs of Seasoned Women; Thema; Wheelhouse Magazine; Xanadu*

By the Same Author

In the Shape of a Woman

Sightings: Poems on Discovery

It Happens As We Speak:
A Feminist Poetics

Contents

One

Lifeline	13
On the Beach	15
Monologue in White Light	17
After Reading *Women on War*	19
War Talk	21
Rookie	22
Sugar Daddy Blues	23
From a Student's Journal	25
Silver Maple	26
Tree, Speak	27
Life in the Forest	28
Blackwater Forest	29
Cemetery Gates	30
In a Time of Changing Light	31
Crazy Jane	32
Swan Nesting	33
Obsidian	34
The Swan's Egg	36
Snow Over Crocus	37
Ducks: An Epilogue	39

Two

On Memory & Other Matters	43
Montauk Journal	44
Breaking Surface	45
To Speak of a River	46
Night Walk, Morning of the Solstice	47
Vesta	49
September Song	50
For My Mother	51
Pegasus	52
Hidden Lake	55
Kaddish	56
Bend in the Road	57
Chinky, a Dog	58
Notes from the Cave	60

Wintering	62
Black Cotton	64
Meditation on a Full Moon	66
To a Gentleman	68
Virgo	69
Heat	70
In Autumn	71

Three

Edenic Sequence	75
1. Apples and trees and spring rain.	75
2. Father has been sleeping for a long time.	76
3. I thought at first it was my father,	77
4. there in the grass	78
5. my brother touched me pulled	79
6. blood in the snow	80
7. something harder than cocoon	81
8. I will not pity this small brown bird	82
9. thinking of miracles the mind	83

Four

Time Out	87
Burnt Umber	88
Woman to Troubadour	89
What She Knows	90
Marigolds	91
Perennial, a Song	92
Blue Night	93
What is Sufficient	94
Notes	95

for Maggie

'Naked I lay,
The grass my bed;
Naked and hidden away'...
And that is what Jane said.

    W.B. Yeats, "Crazy Jane on the Day of Judgment"

jane walks through a green
world in which there is hunger;
in which burned bodies
run towards the camera...

    Kathleen Spivack, *"jane walks"*

One

Lifeline

1.

she won't stop screaming
the air she breathes is red
the air she breathes is

blue

light holds her binds her
red light blinds her
particles and molecules

the ache of birth

2.

the doctor notes the time
ungloves his hands removes
the thin green gown and mask and says

a thing of beauty, wild,
born to pain

3.

so we're all born to pain
I say to myself
picking up the first burnt pot

but why after 43 years this infant
like metal scratched on steel
comes calling in the third bloody

person as if screams, scrubbing
words, distance, could connect
this wired kid to me—

too tired, wise and nearly
beyond compassion
to heed what once were cries

On the Beach

Long Island, July 1996

Difficult to focus, to read,
the sun sinking westward casts a pall
on water still as glass, and flickering
evening shadows. I look skyward—
geese, gulls, something always passes
by—this time, a plane, exploding.

Children sometimes stare at light
through night-time bedroom windows,
or wide-eyed gaze at lamplight
high on hallway ceilings,
then close their eyes, astonished
at the lingering stark frayed image.

Am I so much the child
that I believe whatever blazes, dazzles,
is so utterly my own—that I deny my own
perception, lose the will to speak?
And what have I seen
except a deeply etched reminder

of the true event—a path of light,
a blast, the shattering of lives,
a shattering distinctly etched
but only a reminder:
I never saw the real thing
but see it now on everything that's real.

Difficult to focus, to feel.
To piece metallic shards into a whole.
To feel beyond a fragmentary fear

that leaves the spirit unredeemed and numb.
The sun sinking westward I look skyward.
Is it dawn, this dome of darkness?
Are those stars or burning stone?

Monologue in White Light

I started running when the first bomb fell.
Bomb or crash? Blast, yes.
When the second plane collided with the skyline,
were you still inside? Talk to me. Shock
has turned your eyes to steel your skin to stone
and everywhere a fine grey powder, white light.

Fine grey powder, thin white light on Vesey,
Broadway, Church. What kind of darkness, this?
What kind of light? Any different than your dark-
dark strength and seeming goodness?
Gone, now, the distant screams and dampened sirens,
just this long white stretch of terrible silence.

Terrible, terrible silence.
Are there words for this? Those who say
there are no words deny the spirit, taunt the soul.
Words live within the flesh—
in voweled O-mouth, cut of lip.
Do not bury words like bodies under rubble.

Like bodies under rubble, we try to speak.
I do not know you yet we touch in ways
that make me want to live, like lamplight
falling softly onto shattered glass.
I'm here in the doorway, give me your hand.
The smell of iron is my blood.

Iron, blood, darkness. If I'm to die,
let me admit into my consciousness
only what I'd take with me with joy.
A lasting image: leaf, tree,
pale green light: image
within image, seed within deep seed.

I imagine we're outside by all these pigeons,
flying steep and long, feathered
down and sunk by soot. I believe it's safe
to rest now, rest. I have been running—
through fine grey powder, thin white light—
I started running when the first bomb fell.

After Reading *Women on War*

1.

finally the spaces are filled in
as if there were a map of the world with several territories left blank
as if a group of children came along and filled them in with
      crayons, pens, markers, filled them in with pictures
          and with song—
familiar tools—we've all used them—
but these are voices somehow new, urgently terribly sad

testimony fills the silence
dark faces startled faces filling up the page with whispers,
      warnings, the places and the weapons
         vary
but the terror is the same the unimagined pain the same

a child's eye burning from the inside out
a young man's hand
chopped off   thousands here   millions there
massive open graves

2.

one must stand for many
she's called *comfort woman*   kidnapped first
across the border
placed into a dank dark room
twelve by ten   a basin to clean   a bed to sleep when possible
a long dim hallway leads to
other doors and other rooms and other comfort women

in the hallway thatched and full of stink the soldiers lining up
it is late afternoon it is morning it's the middle
of the night they wait their turn leaning hunched into the wall

getting ready staying warm and hard they take her one at a time
the first time   rupture and blood
the second time ten minutes later third fourth
fifteen in one first night   her lips so swollen
other entry ways must do   soon   those too
swollen and bleeding   she has
a basin for cleaning
a bamboo bed
and space on the floor for a small lamp

3.

numbness in a sea of words   *massive*
genocide   testimonial   comfort
in whom do we find comfort if not in each other
one among continued looming violences must stand for many
as a flower fills the page with long oval leaves
flowing
flowing
outward from a solid center : self : deeper self : connected

I know about pornography and war I claw
my way through fallout image text and lexicon

I change the pronoun *I* to *We*
and close the book
and close the door   behind me

War Talk

what's put been
this into story broken/who
has raised a hand/flag
carved/wind carved sand
more words this
monument of/shake
break remake some/thing
more than one
blast followed/by fellowed
by it comes and came
then name the boon/what
blood/what arm/how
soon the sacred
arm will
gather us and
stars/stares care
less now
unto the goodly word

Rookie

I don't remember the dead boy's name,
the clothing he was wearing
or the street—neon or darkness,
there must have been
a stir or sound, the wind perhaps,
or the humming of the crowd.

Vaguely a river of blood,
moving past the storefront down
the sidewalk, a small black pool
gathered at the curb—and the pen
in my hand, writing, *two in the head
and his neck was slashed.*

I know only the rhythm of detail,
syncopation in a field report,
something to dance to,
a fever of sorts. *Two in the head
and his neck* a river, gathered faces
white with rage—watching.

Sugar Daddy Blues

> From a journalist's interview of a young, homeless, gay man: "For Young Gays on the Streets, Survival Comes Before Pride"; "A string of sugar daddies have briefly taken him in, but his wild ways invariably land him back on the street. He told me he's now in love: 'We're going to have our wedding in Paris, next to a waterfall, with a violin playing…a fairy tale wedding, and we're going to pay for everything ourselves.'"

my sugar daddy's sweet he
gives me beer   food   crack

I suck him day and night and in between

but he don't like my
wild   wild   ways
so I say
screw you   I mean
Fuck YOU sugar daddy
don't need YOUR crap

found me a sweet speakin' brother
street walkin' brother
sittin' by the burned down
fired out rat infested shattered glass
building south of
houston

(So Ho to my white-ass-classy sugar daddy friends)

so what we gonna do
my sweet talking sweet eyed black eyed tired weak and weary dyin'
brother?

we gonna marry
man
do the Jesus thing

and have a
blue house
white fence
picket fence with daffodils and tulips   and
    two kids two dogs one cat
        two cars and one of them
            a shiny SUV

gonna marry like in fairy tales
        a waterfall
        a violin
        a sun shining down on such approving
                faces
        on the streets of sweet Paree!

(and we paid for it ourselves) see

we
still
lookin for a sweet god sinless god
we still lookin for that sugar daddy
lookin for a new law sweet law
lookin for a soft bed sweet bed
safe street sweet street promised land
lollypop and sugardaddy   sugar-daddy   do

From a Student's Journal

dear ms falks I just can't do no writen
to-day   keep thinken of this rat this
slick black thing I run from last

night after eaten up my pork 'n beans
watchen some tv   there he was just run
on out from under-neath the sink I scream

momma! then run like shit
to mommas room   an stop   an see
that mans ass just movin' in her bed

why she scream so soft like that
why so soft   so you see ms falks I just
can't do no writen to-day

Silver Maple

Once upright, a sturdy goddess rising from the grass,
safe it seemed between the sidewalk and the street,
now she wobbles like a small shocked girl.

I touch the sappy pulp, the gaping white exposure
where the skin hangs down in flaps, observe
the tangle of the uprooted roots.

She suffers more I fear from the impact of my touch,
my penetrating eye, than from the car
that tore into her body overnight.

Still, I stay, standing and waiting, standing and waiting,
wanting something not of steel nor stone
nor even human.

No, I say—how can I turn away?
This is not a time of love.

Tree, Speak

I hear you speak, quietly yet clearly through the fog

today it rained for hours
your branches look like wires bent like cat's claws

where have you been? what is it that pains you?
what do you want with me?

from the west a bitter wind
your twigs have thickened into cracked and startled hands

can you hear my voice? who is the one you love?
the night-birds sing along in darkness

whatever grows in winter is my friend

Life In the Forest

All night the nether limbs
pull up against the thrust of gravity.
Old roots, old pain, muffled screams
of fiber rent from stone, shock
of cold stillness.

And of the fallen, by morning,
gathered on the forest floor—
of the dead, we put a match
to the cracked wood,
breath the smoke like incense.

But of those that merely slumber,
we will carve each trunk
into a sacred form—face, neck,
arms, hands, sturdy legs and feet,
teach them how to walk among us,

we whose hands are marked with veins,
whose skin assumes the fabric of a stranger.

Blackwater Forest

after Mary Oliver

The trees in Blackwater Forest
know nothing of pain—
when lightening struck the White Ash

she simply split
and sang of brilliance,
blue light rising from her branches.

To this you are a witness,
tell me I must love what's mortal,
hold it to my bones then let it go—

but I am not a tree I am a woman
and I break.

Cemetery Gates

After Chagall

It is there I want to go—
through the gates,
through a portal overgrown

with scripture,
where words, unknown,
scratched or painted on to stone

bring comfort;
to be in the light, prismatic
drenched in blue

and gentle green;
no need to speak—the dead
have tongues invisible

but palpable—
don't tell me you can't feel
it now—the light,

the humming
fragrance of old trees
among the graves.

In a Time of Changing Light

How much suffering can you stand.
You lean against the wind,
your heavy branches

scrape cement and early grass,
your pitted trunk defiant
at an obtuse angle to the sky.

Cardinals come home to you
like children, unknowing or uncaring
that their tufts of twigs

are lead upon your shoulders. Where
is your one last seed, your dead
leaf blessings to be turned

to earth? Noble oak, sleep now
finally in this time of changing light,
return to darkness, burn.

Crazy Jane

For too long I have carried
you inside me, color and substance
of lead, burden of darkness and dawn.

Now morning cracks the sky,
pulls clouds asunder,
topples every unrelenting oak.

Stones break open—render
seed, scatter, sow and spit out life.
It happens as I speak.

It happens as I thrust
my hand into my heart and demand
your blessing.

Swan Nesting

I watch, wait, would snap her thin white neck,
tell her to get out, quickly—
before the nest is done,
the warm eggs hatched to be destroyed.
Last spring, the giant turtle
took the cygnets down.
Why doesn't she remember?
Stick by small dry stick, mud-thatch,
pebble, twig—a nest as strong
as any human prayer.
Next week she'll have her children,
in three weeks' time they'll all be dead;
twisted instinct keeps her going,
giving, always giving,
complicit in a crazy chain of silently accepting
the way things are.

Obsidian

1.

something happened overnight
though we heard no cry   and the lake
appeared as tranquil as before

we found the nest on a grassy bank
uprooted and shredded,
the swan herself

in hollow reeds
putting stick to stone to mud
in a hurry: she is due

2.

now she sleeps, hidden in the dark marsh
she dreams of small brown beaks
and cloudy water
of how things flutter and
how feathers form in pale-blue shells

one of the six, she imagines,
will survive the spring—
she bobbles in the shade and shallow water

3.

all lost again,
the last one drowned,
tangled up in fishing line
twice around its neck and holding
down its wings—a fish hook
wedged in its jaw

she pulls the feathers off her back,
calls out madly to the wild—*if
only she were human, if only
she were God*

4.

the world shuts down at five o'clock
in early autumn   what's left of spirit
slips

beneath the surface   the swan
herself a leaf or shell
of quiet memory

of silent shapes with small blank eyes
of tethered claws in a world
of kindness

the lake is black
and smooth as glass   the shadows
growing wide and high and very deep

The Swan's Egg

Something good today.
The swan got up and turned an egg. Simple gesture, simple words.

I was standing by the lake, gawking at her nest, its size, the beauty of it all.

Then she pulled herself up and rolled the egg over. She poked and rolled the egg.

So much lately has been fuzzy, violently confused.
Like photographs of torture.

But this seemed real.

So there we were—the swan and me, the oval egg, the father further
      off—and
I kept watching as she lifted up her heavy self, opened up her life
      and let

me in

    to   a universe of sticks and matted feathers
        to oval eggs and   all

her secrets

    (She reaches down with long sleek neck and with her beak she pushes prods and rolls the egg : : a gentle rocking till it tips on to its other side ((the cygnet doing somersaults no doubt)) then sinks

into the nest).

A small space of time : : something moves, is moved, an unexpected slow turning of an egg.

Snow Over Crocus

1.

snow

over crocus

green shoots/penetrating cold

and so many trees down, limbs down, loaded with snow—
some have cracked and fallen into
even deeper
                          snow

the pond is grey under clouds

2.

today the swans are visible—

                  wide wings
flapping as they swoop down squawking

on the surface of the pond—
I'd say that they have swallowed the sun they are so bright but

        no—   I see the sun   winterblinding—
old ice cracking making ovalshapes and teardrop patterns rippling:
        water: water:

3.

he leads, she leads, they circle one another

I'm looking at the thicket where they always build their nest the
place of crush and pull and re-arrange

what stirs?
what is in his heart?   I cannot wait forever

4.

white frost and darkgrey patches where the molecules congeal

I spot a red-spotted black-bird pecking at the ice   scattered
        mallards
oceangulls in softgrey jackets flown in from the sea

: a shimmer in the center of the pond : : still silver water

5.

always the need to break down   chip away at put into play with
and
makeup a story   (in sleep or
                        waking up to new dream)

look: the swans are back   they're walking on the ice he
mounts her feathers flying

into random patterns, cloudforms—

I hold my breath and oh! now they're blackbirds rising
through the snow

   :   : and now they're gone

Ducks: An Epilogue

Only a poet would write about ducks,
see them for their duck-ness, feathers on the water,
little boats with blue-green flags sailing off,
or coming on to shore with a waddle or a limp.

I sat on my beach, a fine day in May.
I could not write, or rather would not, given all
the drivel that I knew would claim my hand.
Then came the ducks, who stood and stared at me
as still as ancient stone. *Move* I said, silently of course,
not wanting to disturb their sacred aura.
Move. Come to me. If you do you are most
certainly ambassadors of God.

They budged neither feather nor an inch
no matter how intensely I returned their gaze.
It then became clear, they had come to test my faith.
I walked back home more humble than I'd been
in a long time. Before I went inside,
I looked back to see, like four vagrant thoughts,
the ducks had followed me.

It's a funny life, you know.
And stranger when you think of what will move us.

Two

On Memory & Other Matters

what resides here
what flutters in the light of still standing water—
oxygen and darkness   small fish that dart and whirl

(if you swim on a moonless night
you can see the water flash with your movements—)

I want to remember
all that lives on the ocean's floor
but I also want more

there is a state where things   are not sufficient
where a name is something written on a soul
that needs to be said

that needs to be said to someone who hears

Montauk Journal

I have long thought the universe alive, all forms equal:
cup, cloud, bird, tree, a child's ball rolling down a hillside
in Kentucky or Japan, the stars in mimic motion;
here now at heart-center, center heart, dream machine
of mundi spirit, spiritus mundi, call and break of passing
fading, crashing plash on purpled sand and broken stone
and back again; witness how the silence comes alive,
what never was was only silence in a blind dumb deathlike
absence, abiding in the earth's deep pit of bone and blood
of beast that beats in steadfast rhythm; change me, change me,
cruel crustacean rock and weed, pretend to know and render
what my soul does to the sea, as if the earth itself were bathed
in fine sheer gleaming sheen of animated matter making
whitefoam whiter in the spitting out of open pockets under
undercurrent urge and urge of ceaseless silent song.

Breaking Surface

if I were to try   to write again
it would be prayer   the form—

                              jazz

tuneful, mournful, a celebration of what is
for the moment taking off—

a medium, an ink
where the fruit of disaster
and the fruit of goodness
cluster and groan

a hand on my foot
rope around my ankle—
systole, diastole

rising
to the surface clutching bone breaking stone

this is my fear and this
is my salvation

To Speak of a River

I used to live by the river; for fifteen years the river had frozen
and thawed, frozen and thawed
and I had risen every morning to a moon slipping
westward and to stars that re-arranged themselves,
drifting.

The river is a fine old teacher, brown god, sightless,
formed by impulse, shifting boundary.
The river has served, served well—nurtured geese
and ducks and swans, provided soft sea moss
and sturdy stones for reeds.

Do you know where the ducks sleep? On the far side of the river,
hidden in the hollow of the brush;
sometimes, though,
they merely float on the current in the night.

Night Walk, Morning of the Solstice

1.

I call to my daughter through her sleep.
My voice must be the wind to her, her mind a harp,
for she hums the notes of a song we used to sing.

I call again: *Karen.* I think she hears, for under
folds of sheets and woolen spreads, she stirs,
draws up long limbs closer to her chest.

When she was two, I carried her from bed
to the comfort of the rocker, when she was eight,
I'd walk her to the couch, her star-like hand

pressed warm in mine.
Now from the windy hall I call her name.
She moves more deeply into sleep, turns her head away.

2.

Outside, it might as well be midnight at half passed six.
The moon is slipping into darkness.
Once I would have followed,

but I am seeking tenderness, something
that the night won't give, something found perhaps
in subtle demarcations: street, tree, frozen river

field beyond where wild ducks are waiting, waiting
for the light, or warmth, or for the seed
I bring them every morning.

The moon has vanished into darkness.
I move further into shadow and my daughter
into sleep.

3.

If she were up and walked with me,
I would show her how the clouds rise slowly off the river,
tell her how the sun breaks fully without warning, sometimes,

that age has made me see these things and think these things,
has made me mourn the passing of each day.
And yes if she were with me on this morning of all mornings

I would tell her that I'm only
sometimes lonely, that I fear the ache of rupture,
but I need to let her go.

I scatter fine crushed corn and broken pellets on the river bank:
mallard, pintail, blue-winged teal: everything
is crystal, everything is still.

Vesta

1.

A woman bringing fire from her mother's hearth
to light her own in her own new home.
I like this story, an ancient Roman ritual, and tell
it to my daughter though I get it wrong on the first try.
I say the mother *gives* the flame, hands
it to her daughter like a bag of apples
or cash against emergency.
But a daughter needs to choose before she takes,
to use her hands as she sees fit, for culling grain
or spreading seed, replacing broken d-strings
on an old guitar. And what about a knife or a gun?
Within arm's reach. Scale fish, sculpt form,
ward off anyone who comes into the house unasked.
Let me not be one of those unasked.

2.

News from afar of war; nearer too, political unease.
Signs and omens read me, compel me to the story's end:
women bringing fire from hearth to hearth
to the center of the city. I tell this to my daughter,
pacing like a lynx in the room I gave her
long ago. "We must," I tell her, "separate, as completely
as the morning you were born, your raging flesh
rent fast from mine. I'll find you when the war is over,
by the wounded bridge or in the last abandoned building.
Now let me hold you, briefly, just for a moment, just
for all eternity. My spirit's blazing, burning in and out
my own wild life: feel it, hold it, keep it in your
mind's eye, heart's core, deepest dream cupped and
closed and open, then move on: go with it, go with it, go."

September Song

At eight years old I played Chopin
on my mother's grand piano.
Two canaries, separate,
caged on either side of a large bay window,
sang as my fingers flew across the keys.

I could not play on Yom Kippur.
I could do nothing on that somber day
but roam from room to darkened room.
Upstairs, my father busy with his suit
and grey striped tie; my mother fierce,
maddened by a law she neither
liked nor understood.

The birds, unconnected to our household
god would chirp and flutter when I stole
into the room. At noon I brought them seed,
promising a song at sundown.
By two we would wait no longer.
I pulled up the shade, sat down at the keys
and we all burst into a sweet September song.

My father drew the shades, wound a sheet
around each cage. My mother knew my pain,
so much her own she pulled me to the floor
and dragged me by my braided hair
to the confines of my room.
Later, in the dark, when ignorance
and sleep swept the corners of our home,
I crept back out.

How good to run my hands across the cool
and waxy wood, my silent fingers sliding
on the black, along the white.

For My Mother

I remember being hit
till my skin turned thick
and people thought me shy or cold.

I remember seconals, tuinals,
dexedrine, amphetamine, your mood
shifts named on plastic phials.

When you slashed your wrists
I held your hand, sopped
the blood with Kleenex.

I'm 43, you're 64, and you ask me
if I ever loved you, mother.

I remember fear and need,
but I don't remember love.

Pegasus

1.

born of the blood
of Medusa

a blade
to her throat

gave me vision
I saw   my life

through that rupture,
carried

on a scream
then falling with

the weight
of rage to earth

2.

I push my finger
deep into the ground

to feel for hope   that's all I know

how to probe, wait
for indentations to fill up with rain

3.

the surface of a lake
is often cloudy—still, I drink

it is said that poetry resides
here, its crystals

can be seen reflected
in the sun— it must be so—

for no sooner do I drink
than I am filled with song

4.

slow are my wings to open
slower still

are hoof and haunch
to bear the weight of form

5.

On a clear night
when the constellations

open up like flattened pages
you may remember

you may even
make connections

believing in a sacred order
to the universe

if you see me hanging upside-down
in heaven, look again

I can be
my mother's daughter—

I swear
I never will

Hidden Lake

Like a small brown robin
or a wren,
I have come to a place

only God could imagine,
a lake, a clump
of trees,

some broken branches dangling
in the shallow.
Show me how to surrender,

to feel the hungry shock
of it—from stone
to stone

from bondage into breath—
I need to learn to love and lose
the smallest

grain of sand,
of marrow, root and bone,
an opening, a home.

Kaddish

I lift the wine to my lips,
l'chaim—
and drink to life my father's
death, twenty years
of ugly death

the wine his blood,
drained before they buried him,
before the reading
of the Kaddish—
words they would not

let me say beside
the hollow comfort of his grave—
Kaddish came from men
so daughters didn't
count—

twenty years later I begin to count
yisgadal, v'yiskadash, yisbarach,
v'yishtabach…
I lift the wine to my lips,
l'chaim.

Bend in the Road

I will walk with you to where the road ends, to the clump of pine,
where wild weed runs helter-skelter to the sea.
I'll turn then, continue to the shore line, leaving you
to journey on in peace.

Is this your hand, my father, dead now twenty-five years?
Once I wished you'd hold me, embrace me as
you do so now. How cold you seemed,
my own flesh soft, warm.

Here the road ends.
Here's the stone that bears your name.
I clasp my hands, slide my fingers one inside
beside the other, sunk into a temple-tangled prayer:

shallow water, sand bar, shell-shard song:
how easily—too easily—we fill the in-between.

Chinky, a Dog

Chinky was our Pekingese, a Chinese breed
with silky hair, a smashed-in face
and gorgeous dark eyes.
My mother named him Chinky.
This was not politically correct, but understand
it was the fifties in a neighborhood
of upper middle—Jewish—class whites.

We never walked him, just let him out the door
into the street down Chevy Chase and Kent
where kind Mrs. Leibow threw him scraps of meat.
I'd often have to call him home, and standing
high on Avon Road, where ivy-covered Tudors
sank into the rolling landscape, yell *Chinky!
Cheeeeeeeeeee-nnnnnnnn-keeeeeeeeeee!*

Oh I was not myself. Not a chubby ten year old
in itchy skirt and cotton blouse.
I was a megaphone. I was ALL VOICE.
The soul of the earth. Chinky! Here boy!
*He is bounding up the hill, his long ears flapping
back like rabbit ears flattened in the wind.
A furry brown bullet darting up the road.*

No one told me I was bad or wrong.
The Azaleas kept blooming and the snow
kept falling as the years unfolded.
Then Chinky died—he must have, I assumed—
but I never knew exactly how or when.
He didn't make it home one day
no matter how long I called and cried.

And then the neighborhood changed.
The Nazareths moved in on Radnor Road,
the Mohammedovs on Aberdeen, and after that
a steady stream of Wu, Yoon, Rodriguez and Zhu.
My voice grew dull, lost in the babble, lost within my loss.
Alone, I'd whisper *Chinky*, the name now twisted into shame
like the kinks of my ponytail gripped by thick blue bands.

Notes from the Cave

1.

Mid-November, damp, cold,
redleaf, goldleaf, crushed on asphalt,
frost on the branches, frost in the grass,
and the river with that waxy look
it gets before the snow.

Still it is not yet winter,
and sufficient light fills the house,
light enough at five o'clock
for thinking, dreaming.

2.

I found a child's ragdoll on the beach,
sand matted in her hair, her left foot
torn and tangled into broken shells.

I left her there, but took the image home
like sunburn on my back, the wind like history
beating time against my skin.

3.

I am reminded of a huge old volume
in the dialect of Plato,
something in translation about light,
and caves, and insubstantial shadows,
the word *platonic* running
madly through my mind while my fingers
skim the page for something real.

4.

The drive to make connections,
walking through the desert from desire
to despair. *The drive to connect,*
my hand moving closer
to the clustered fruit
I have wanted all my life to hold
in the smooth round darkness of my palm.

5.

At the end of the mind, a shadow.
An orchid rooted in the earth,
one wild star blazing among many.
Delirious, spontaneous,
we just reach out, amazed
at our undoing.

6.

Late November, damp, cold, redleaf,
goldleaf, stained on asphalt.
Still it is not yet winter,
and sufficient light fills the house.
I will assess the worth of shadows,
try to scrawl a word of truth, begin
to make sense, refuse
to be trapped,
dismantle, unbridle, rekindle,
redouble, untrouble the trouble of love.

Wintering

1.

stretch of dune, pink shrub at Robert Moses
the roadway dotted with signs   *please don't feed the wildlife*

how many killed   the signs give numbers

sand shifts
the ocean   is vast   is blue
is what I need to breath: someone showed me once
how
to breath under water though she too
now is dead   metaphors are useful
though essentially
untrue

2.

if I surrender to a presence
                        some call *God*
will I finally lose this wretched wanting?

but surrender to a power called *He?*

I confess I have resented
that word
that power
that certainty solemnity indemnity masculinity

3.

must I separate the male god
from you the man in bed
beside me?

there is a blue light here
in the darkness

red light   down here
shredded white—

how different
is your spirit from mine

4.

love—perhaps disaster—in the quiet
shallow of the pond   just outside my door

I am afraid of you   wide-mouth moon
angry that you touch me   this way

wind over pond   dark clouds, ice

I believe that I can change you, driven
as I am toward morning.

Black Cotton

1.

I think he is an army vet,
that young man gazing out to sea,
he's standing with his back to me
but I know that gaze.
His tee-shirt's tattered cotton,
frayed and faded black,
the left sleeve hollow, flapping.
What I think, see: *torso, body without arm.*
He must have been wounded in action,
in the hills of Afghanistan
or by a roadside bomb in Iraq.
He's home now from the war, adjusting.
I ought to talk to him,
tell him that despite our awful presence...
but now a young blond woman's
running up beside him.
There you are! she laughs,
he smiles, and with his one
good arm he pulls and holds her
close against his heart.
And now I think he's not a wounded
soldier after all.
He works the late shift in a factory,
his arm mangled by machine.
The lovers walk away.
The day, I note, is hot and dry as dust
and long thin clouds drift slowly out to sea.

2.

I read a poem once, about a dying plant,
the stem and leaves were spotted with decay,
the roots crumbling into sticky blackness.

The speaker of the poem lived alone
in a cramped two rooms of a downtown walkup.
A brutal day in August—it was 99 degrees—
he lugged the plant, pot and all,
down the six steep flights to the dumpster.
He threw it in, then trudged back up
the endless steps of burning steel.
That night he went back down
to reclaim the dying plant.
The poem concludes, "I was that
lonely."

Meditation on a Full Moon

For Gary

1.

The moon is lonely,
if to be lonely is to burn so brightly
in a dark December sky that the stars—
the ones we used to wish upon—are gone.

We who are guided by the moon
test the limits of our sanity and other loves,
we trace curves that have been there always,
find comfort in recognition.
Migratory birds in flight know this,
we have seen them as shadows on giant stones.

2.

I had lunch with a friend who told me he was lonely.
He did not blurt out "I am lonely,"
as we stared across the table
at each other's clothes. He smiled, frowned,
little wrinkles crept about his eyes
when he chanced to laugh.

He sang once, in the middle of a conversation
just started singing how he can't be changed.
I stopped speaking, put his words
into the rhythm of a poem, then moved
my cup to the center of my plate.
We spoke at last of what it's like to live alone.

3.

I am walking by the river and look up at the moon,
gaze openly and long, without the fear of burning.
If I close my eyes, perhaps I'll see
a bright light remaining,
etched into my sight. Or at least a shadow,
a little less darker than the dark.

To a Gentleman

enter gently this good day,
unfold the folds of velvet rose

but neither mourn nor rage
against its stony thorn—

there too dawn delivers;
let light fall, fill the space

between these thighs, where gods
have drunk and danced for years

without our help—come, sweet sir,
day will not be seized.

Virgo

I look into the mirror, where the future looms
in present tense, then walk out of the house
into the stark day.

I want to prod the moment open like a soft jewel,
whisper intimations, unmask the mask of *now*
and put it on to forget.

Trees know how to do this—the massive oak
with her thick black branches. Gnarled and thick
and hard. So sexual, so open, legs and oval crevice.

And standing on an island in the middle of the road,
a sapling maple. No new leaves though the old
dry dead ones have finally fallen off.

Walk up close to: examine: round swollen buds.
Just last Tuesday they were tight and brown,
now they burn with blistering green.

(Still the opalescent essence,
safely hidden).
Come up close to, walking to take with.

Heat

I am waiting for the heat to melt me
for the sun to sink more deeply in my bones
I will be flattened   beached
bronzed

if the sun is male   so be it
let his violet rays penetrate and soothe me

or let the sun be woman
she too will take me as I open to her tongue

the warm wind passes through me like
another language
stunned   I begin the work of life

In Autumn

A handful of pansies, one stray rose,
linger, despite the last few night-time frosts
and rush of weeds I never pulled.

My garden! A wonder you are still alive,
like me, at forty, full of lustful humming,
but deeper, lighter, stronger than before.

I am spreading like the sun,
my life a life of weeds and seeds,
stiff stalks and petals, promises and wind.

Three

Edenic Sequence

1.

Apples and trees and spring rain.
Eternal April, when my spirit swells
with the swelling of the earth

when small stiff buds work silently,
invisibly, knowing what they need
they grab and cling.

Later when the earth is wiser,
after the long spring rain, and wind
and trembling—sprout, leaf, tree.

And while all this love
(can I call it love?) and lust and life
go on, continue through an elsewhere

nod or yawn; through snow, ice, thaw,
bud, wild bloom—the awful penetration
and the

        not death, for death is good,
        old dead leaves left dangling
        on the branches

        are soon urged on—go now—
        off with you—
        by small new forms
                not death: Mask.

Apples and trees and spring rain,
where is my mother, my father, my God.

2.

Father has been sleeping for a long time.
I can tell when he is dreaming,
his body pales, darkens.

Once he called my mother's name,
his arms drawn tightly to his chest—as if
to stay the ache of absence.

I tried to wake him, whispering my mother
was not far away, but he fell into a deeper
sleep that looked like peace.

Mother comes and goes across the garden's
boundaries, sometimes to the city
where there's rumor of impending change.

At night she lies beside my father,
a hand on his shoulder, fingers to his face.
I've heard her cry.

3.

I thought at first it was my father,
newly wakened, working in the field,
his shirt sleeves clinging to his arms.

But as I neared the furrow
where he turned the earth, I saw the man
I once had called my brother.

Wild child. We used to laugh and dance,
slip in stony streams. Dark child,
who loved me till he feared

I'd grown into a woman. How I hate
that fear. Now I watch him, watch him,
all day long and through the night.

4.

    there   in the grass
    in the silver light   weak but clear
    of autumn

    centered in the blade
    substantive

    an oval eye in the long thin blade

    I will sleep here tonight
    for the eye   in the center

    is closed

5.

my brother touched me
pulled the thin white cotton
from my shoulders

and in the dark
light of morning I knew
lust—

sand in the desert
the sycamore
singing   this—   joy

his hand on my breast
his hand moving slowly
like a river

down my belly—
and when he entered me
it seemed a thousand

times his swelling fitting
perfectly
the sycamore singing

and the sand—
I began to remember
the day we were born

6.

blood in the snow
first thing that I see

when I step out of the house
dialogue of crimson and dull innocence

similar I think to the heart
though the heart is darker

opens to the cold
then closes when the wind blows

blood in the snow, tracks
across a field where the hunted

and the hunter crouch in matted fur
snow blown by northwest winds

blurs the space between them
one of them is me

I need to find a clear path—
green grass—far from home

7.

something harder than cocoon
has grown around me
thicker than an egg-shell

darker than the yellow-brown
of a nut-shell
pebbled on the inside

from the exploration of my hand
years and years, my nails
grow longer, lovely

as a knife-edge drawing blood

8.

I will not pity this small brown bird
feathers and flesh, torn

by some relentless local beast,
in a changed and changing landscape—

snowdrift, ice-patch, inconsistent river,
what to me is one small bird?

what to anyone is one small bird?

we have come too often to this place
denied too long our own small truths

today is a day of ice—brilliant,
sure and strong

9.

thinking of miracles   the mind
traveling the surface of a lake

frozen over   blanketed with snow
though silver-blue in patches

where the wind has swept it bare

thinking of miracles
skirting the perimeter   rooting in the dark edge

this could also be a river   this
could also be a heart closed long enough

to know   the beauty of winter
and stillness and ice

Four

Time Out

If I never write again I will be happy,
continue easily to clean the house
and teach and play piano,
swim an hour every other day;
but no more words—worn, torn,
waiting for redemption.

Happy, I think,
lowering my hips and thighs
into the glassy pool, the water
smacking cold at first but growing warm
with every stroke and lap.
I've rearranged my chromosomes,

my cells abound with long lost
beauty and with power.
Happy not to write or even love again
if that's what's needed.
To hell with poems of birds and trees,
of mythic wings and knotty roots:

give me quiet fire in the flesh,
the cool blue comfort of the pool.

Burnt Umber

In the chaos of the bed I reach for you,
find shadows, forests, sand I think
with joy the landscape of your flesh.
But when was sand like this? Burnt umber,
blazing under brutal sun.
I seek darkness—

a cavern cool enough
to turn the ashes of my skin to stone.
I look into your eyes: they too
are stone, artifacts that bring desire
to her knees, begging. History
folds upon itself, our stories

tangled like the arms legs thighs
and hips that we believed since birth
could join with ease. Will we ever say
these words—hope, love, innocence—
as if they were not markers in a game
but tokens of our true desire?

The building is on fire.
I am naked in this bed, and in your arms
give in to all that we remember and forget.

Woman to Troubadour

You have sung to me for centuries,
it is written in the deepest
furrows of this tree—
while layer after layer, I have
shed unwanted garments
I am stripped down to truth.

It seems you have seduced me, looked
into my soul and traced the smooth
dark contours of my breasts,
your fingers on the strings of wooden
instruments—linger
by the crevice of my sex.

Until at last this tree, rooted
in her own sweet secrets, relinquishes
her grasp and urges me to fall—
into the fierce stark rhythm
of your language,
the pulse and power of your song.

What She Knows

A man has planted something
far inside me, an image or a form,
brown seed, word, deed—all things
become the same in this chamber—
and since the time he planted it
a dreamy rush of pleasure

has taken hold. First of my heart,
pumping all the while my own
blood, pumping through my veins
into my brain into the textured
lining of my lungs where
song is born,

pressing through my breasts,
rounded nipples, flowing hips, desire
in my belly running idly down my thighs.
I part my legs and touch myself:
is this the magic of translation
or his hand?

A searing rod or root keeps re-entering
my flesh *my language is my body I am
very much alive.*

Marigolds

I will walk for hours, thinking
of marigolds to plant this spring,
imagining the small frail faces
tumbling out of plastic trays,
their laughter as I nudge them up,
tuck them into open earth.

Planting they say is hope,
but marigolds won't thrive
on hope alone, will never spread
to flames of wild joy—without
the slow sweet work
of sun and solid earth.

They are blessedly unconscious,
most tender, loyal friends—orange,
gold, tangled rhythms in a garden-patch
where just below the surface,
in pebbled dewy darkness, new roots
thicken and split, hand grips hand.

Perennial, a Song

Because it is spring I will try again,
because I love silence and darkness
and the coming of light   because I still
seek signs, wanting to believe
that you too, miles away
have risen.

I stumble half asleep to a window left
open all night, part the thin white curtain,
damp from last night's snow   I heard
a song in my sleep, perhaps the snow
fell on me like music, bedding
down the earth.

Have you seen the snow?
Have you heard strange songs too difficult
to sing because they're so close to the truth?
I wake this morning without husk,
without a mask, rooted in silence and darkness,
moving again toward the light.

Blue Night

I would rather sleep than write,
would rather dream, sink with ease
into a vision merely given,
a leaf driven giddily by wind,
weightless and falling,
starlike and dumb.

But tonight I cannot sleep,
anchored to the hours
like a paperweight of brass,
resigned to sift against all gravity
sand, stone, weed, dreams—
and pull them back,

back, tide-like from yours   :   :   blue night,
background of cobalt on paper   glint
of early morning in a flash   how to enter
into change and walk out of   the image
as it works its way in me   I am
taken to a place

where walls and time my fear of love
my fear of you are crushed
in the tearing wind.

What is Sufficient

One room: a window facing east,
sunlight on the table where I sit thinking
how time moves so slowly as I age,
as I read, slowly, entering the text,
sunlight on my neck
penetrates the network of small bone.

I would like to see you, speak with you,
before I'm finished reading,
before the sunlight fades
to vacant shadow and I fall asleep,
someone else inhabiting the room, reading,
words on the page arranged into a story,

your story, my story, your room, my room,
the first and last the only
true commitment.

Notes

"Jane walks through a green world..." "jane walks" in Kathleen Spivack, *The Jane Poems*. Doubleday & Company, Inc. Garden City, New York 1974, p. 30.

"After Reading *Women on War*": My title refers to the anthology *Women on War: An International Anthology Of Writings From Antiquity To the Present*, edited by Daniela Gioseffi; The Feminist Press, New York, 1993. Part 2 refers to Maria Rosa Henson's memoir, "Comfort Women," included in the anthology.

"Sugar Daddy Blues," takes text from "For Young Gays on the Streets, Survival Comes Before Pride," *The New York Times*, June 27, 2004.

"Blackwater Forest": See Mary Oliver's, "In Blackwater Woods," in *New and Selected Poems*. Beacon Press, Boston. 1992.

"Cemetery Gates" refers to Marc Chagall's "The Cemetery Gates," 1917. Oil on canvas, 87x68.5 cm. Musee National d'Art Modern, Centre Georges Pompidou.

"Black Cotton," part 2 refers to Theodore Roethke's poem, "The Geranium," though in his poem it was a "cretin of a maid" who threw the plant into the trash can.

"Edenic Sequence": This poem grew out of a conversation with a friend who had been moved by the book, *A Course in Miracles*. He said the book mentions that while Adam was placed into a deep sleep when his rib was removed, the bible (i.e. the Judiac Old Testament) never tells of his awakening; therefore all of humanity is apparently the embodiment of Adam's unconscious. In response to this premise, I imagined Eve, who—having been formed of the rib while Adam slept—must be living outside the dream; then I thought of her children, and specifically, her daughter, in whose voice I wrote the sequence.

www.ingramcontent.com/pod-product-compliance
Lightning Source LLC
Chambersburg PA
CBHW071023080526
44587CB00015B/2475